A

SAINT

FOR YOUR NAME

SAINTS FOR GIRLS

A SAINT FOR YOUR NAME

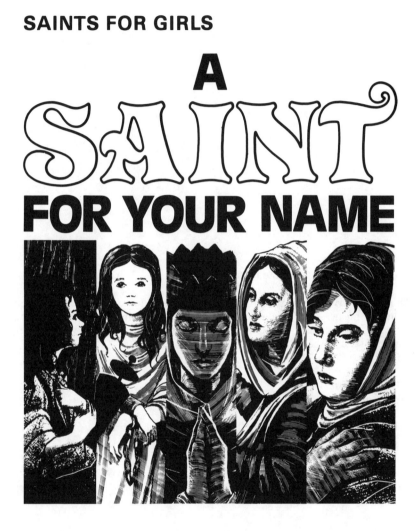

Albert J. Nevins, M.M.

ILLUSTRATED BY JAMES McILRATH

Our Sunday Visitor, Inc.
Huntington, Indiana 46750

920
Nev

12336

ISBN: 0-87973-321-7
Library of Congress Catalog Card Number: 79-92502

Published, printed, and bound in the United States of America

In This Book:

Preface: BEFORE YOU BEGIN • page 7
Part One: SAINTS FOR GIRLS • page 9
Part Two: NAMES IN THIS BOOK • page 91

Pictures

St. Agnes • page 12

St. Ann • 16

St. Bernadette • 20

St. Catherine of Siena • 23

St. Clare of Assisi • 26

St. Dorothy • 31

St. Elizabeth • 33

St. Elizabeth of Hungary • 35

St. Elizabeth Ann Seton • 37

St. Frances Xavier Cabrini • 41

St. Frances of Rome • 44

St. Genevieve • 46

St. Germaine • 49

St. Helena • 53

St. Joan of Arc • 56

St. Lucy • 61

St. Mary Magdalene • 63

St. Margaret of Scotland • 65

St. Martha • 67

Blessed Virgin Mary • 69

St. Monica • 72

St. Rose of Lima • 78

St. Teresa of Avila • 82

St. Thérèse of Lisieux • 85

Before You Begin

It is a Christian custom that when a baby is baptized it is given the name of a saint who is to be the protector and model for the new Christian. Later at Confirmation the child chooses to take the name of another saint who is also a model and protector.

Since there are many thousands of saints, this book lists only those whose names seem more popular. There are also different ways a saint's name can be spelled and these forms are found under the original name and in the listing at the back of this book. Often there is more than one saint with the same name. This book gives only those who are best known. Some names of girls (Rosemarie, Marianna, etc.) are made of two saints' names and the first part is taken to be the principal saint.

After each saint's name is the language from which the name comes and its meaning. The date after each name is the feast day of the saint and thus it is also the name day of those called after the saint. Such a day should be treated something like a birthday — a special day on which you should be remembered and you should remember your saint.

Although this is a book for girls, many girls' names are the feminine form of a male name. If there is no saint with the girl's name, reference is made to the male saint. More details about this saint can be found in the companion book of boys' names.

It is hoped that you will try to become like the saint after whom you have been named, remembering the saint in your prayers and imitating her love for Jesus.

Part One:

Saints for Girls

(alphabetical listing)

Abigail (*Hebrew:* The Father Is Happy)

Other Forms: Abbie, Abby, Gail, Gale

There is no saint by this name, but there is an Abigail in the Bible. She was an intelligent and attractive woman who was married to a wealthy man named Nabal. David, who was not yet king of Israel, sent emissaries to Nabal, who treated them unkindly. David took some soldiers and went after Nabal to punish him. Before he found Nabal, David met Abigail, who talked him out of vengeance. Shortly afterwards, Nabal died and David took Abigail as his wife.

Ada (*Teutonic:* Happy)   Apr. 23

Another Form: Adalberta

Ada is the diminutive and feminine form for St. Adalbert (April 23), who is one of the patrons of Poland and Bohemia. He became a priest and bishop and was put to death in 997 while doing missionary work in what is now Hungary and Poland.

Adele (*Teutonic:* Noble)   Dec. 24

Other Forms: Adalie, Adela, Adelaide, Adelheid, Adelina, Adeline, Aline, Della

St. Adele was a princess, daughter of Dagobert, King of the Franks. With her sister, Irmina, she founded a monastery at Treves where she spent her life serving the poor. She lived in the early part of the 8th Century. Because of her great charity, she was honored as a saint after death.

ST. ADELAIDE   (Dec. 16)

St. Adelaide was an empress. She was a Burgundian princess who married the King of Italy. After his death and much persecution she wed Otho, the great German emperor. She did much good for the Church and was called the "Peacemaker of Europe." She died in 999 while living in a monastery in Alsace.

ST. AGNES

Adria *(Latin:* Dark)   Dec. 2

Other Forms: Adriana, Adrienne

St. Adria was in a group of ten Christians who were arrested during the persecution of the Emperor Valerian (254-259) in Rome. They were put to death in various ways. St. Adria became a martyr when she was killed by scourging for refusing to deny her religion.

Agatha *(Greek:* Good)   Feb. 5

Other forms: Agathe, Agathy

St. Agatha is one of the ancient martyrs of the Church whose name is listed in the First Eucharistic Prayer of the Mass. She is a patroness of nurses and is prayed to as a protector against fire. She is said to have lived in Sicily and to have been very beautiful and rich. When she was a child she consecrated her life to God. During the persecution of the Emperor Decius, a greedy judge sought to marry her and gain her fortune. She refused and was arrested. Because she was a Christian, the judge had her tortured, first by beating, then by cutting off her breasts. Finally, she was rolled naked over burning coals and died praising God (c. 251).

Agnes *(Greek:* Pure)   Jan. 21

Other Forms: Agnella, Agnete, Agnita, Ines, Inez, Neysa, Nina, Ninette, Rachel

The name of St. Agnes is remembered in Eucharistic Prayer I of the Mass. She is a very popular martyr of the early Church. She was only thirteen years old when arrested. She was ordered to deny God and marry a pagan. She refused both commands and was beheaded. She died about 300 in Rome. The daughter of the Emperor Constantine had a church built over her grave. Agnes is usually painted with a lamb at her feet and the sword of martyrdom in her hand.

Albina (*Latin:* White)   Dec. 16

Other Forms: Alba, Bianca, Blanche

St. Albina was a Christian maiden who was put to death in Palestine for her faith during the persecution of the Roman Emperor Decius. Her relics were later brought to Italy and enshrined in a church near Naples.

Alberta (Feminine of Albert,   Nov. 15
Teutonic: Illustrious)

Another Form: Albertina

St. Albert the Great, a German teacher and Doctor (Teacher) of the Church, is the principal saint of this name.

Alessandra (Feminine of Alexander,
Greek: Helper of Men)

Other Forms: Aleth, Alex, Alexandra, Alexandrina, Alexis, Cassandra, Sandra (see)

There are many saints with the name of Alexander. One was St. Alexander, the first bishop of Constantinople after its name was changed from Byzantium. He fought against the heretic Arius and defended the Catholic Faith. His feast is Aug. 28. St. Alexander Briant (Dec. 1) was an English priest who was arrested for his faith, put to the rack and other tortures under Queen Elizabeth, and finally hanged on Tyburn Hill, Dec. 1, 1581.

Alice (*Teutonic:* Noble Cheer)   June 11

Other Forms: Aleydis, Alicia, Alisa, Alison, Alix, Alyce, Alys, Elissa, Else, Ilsa, Illse

St. Alice of Schaerbeck was a Cistercian nun in a monastery near Brussels, Belgium. After a very holy life she died about the year 1300.

14

Alma *(Latin:* Loving) Aug. 22

This is a title of the Blessed Virgin Mary, *Alma Mater,* Loving Mother. The feast of Mary, Queen and Mother, is celebrated Aug. 22.

Amanda (Feminine of Amandus, Feb. 6
Latin: Worthy of Love)

St. Amandus was born in the west of France where he became a monk at the abbey of St. Martin of Tours. At the request of the king, he went as a missioner to Flanders and Holland. He founded many churches and monasteries and made many conversions. Because of this, he is usually pictured holding a church in his hands. He died in 684 and is called the Apostle of Flanders.

Amata (Feminine of Amatus, *Latin:* Loved) Sept. 13

Other Forms: Amy, Aimee

St. Amatus was born in Grenoble, France. As a young man, he entered a monastery and became a priest. However, the life was not strict enough for him so he withdrew and became a hermit. His holiness and reputed gift of miracles drew many people to his retreat. He converted a rich and powerful baron who built St. Amatus a monastery, which he governed until his death in 627.

Anastasia *(Greek:* Who Will Rise Again) Dec. 24

Other Forms: Stacey, Stasia, Stathia, Statia

St. Anastasia is one of the women whose name is listed in the First Eucharistic Prayer of the Mass. She was a noble woman who after the death of her husband used her wealth to aid Christian victims of the persecution that was taking place in Rome. She was arrested under the Emperor Diocletian (A.D. 304), tortured and burned to death. An ancient church in Rome is named in her honor.

ST. ANN

Andrea (Feminine of Andrew, *Greek:* Manly)   Nov. 30

St. Andrew was an Apostle, brother of St. Peter. He is a patron of fishermen and women who wish to be mothers.

Angela (*Latin:* Angel)   Jan. 16

Other Forms: Angel, Angelica, Angelina, Angelique, Angelita

St. Angela Merici was the foundress of the worldwide order of Ursuline Sisters. She was born about 1474 in Italy into a well-to-do family. When she was 15, both of her parents died, and she went to live with an uncle. She joined the Franciscan Third Order, lay people who live in the world and practice the spirit and rule of St. Francis of Assisi. She fasted on bread and water, and slept on boards. She made many pilgrimages about Italy and in 1524 went to the Holy Land. She was concerned about the paganism she saw growing in Italy, particularly as it affected family life. To provide for the education of future Christian mothers, she founded a community of women in 1535, placing it under the patronage of St. Ursula, an early Christian martyr. She died in 1540.

Ann (*Hebrew:* Grace)   July 26

Other Forms: Anita, Anna, Annabel, Annabella, Anne, Annette, Hannah, Nan, Nancy, Nanette, Niñon

The Bible does not tell us anything about St. Ann, mother of the Blessed Virgin Mary, so we have to depend upon the tradition of the early Church. According to one work of those times, Ann was married to a man named Joachim, who like her was of the tribe of Judah. For many years the couple were childless, so they prayed and fasted, begging God for a child. At last a baby came, and they named her Mary. Devotion to St. Ann was very popular in the Eastern Church, where there are three feasts in her honor. The Emperor Justinian built a great basilica to her in Constantinople. Gradually devotion to St. Ann spread through the Western Church. Many shrines were built to her, and the best known to Americans is that of St. Anne de Beaupré in Canada where thousands of pilgrims go each year and where many miracles are said to have taken place through her intercession. Her statues usually show an older woman with a small girl (Mary).

Antonia (Feminine of Anthony, *Greek:* Priceless)

Other Forms: Antoinette, Antonina, Tanya, Toni, Tonia

The saint most honored by this name is St. Anthony of Padua (June 13), one of the most popular Franciscan saints. There is a Blessed Antonia Gainaci (1407-1507) who was a Dominican Sister of great holiness. Her feast day is Oct. 27.

Audrey (*Greek:* Noble Maiden)   June 22

This is a form of Etheldra (*see*).

Barbara (*Greek:* Stranger)   Dec. 4

St. Barbara is honored by the Church as a virgin and martyr who died about 235 A.D. According to legend, Barbara grew up in a pagan household where great honor was paid the Roman gods. Despite the fact that she was carefully watched, she took secret instructions in Christianity and was baptized. When her father learned of her conversion, he was furious. Barbara fled into the mountains but was recaptured by her father and turned over to the prefect who had been charged by the Emperor Maximinus to stamp out Christianity in the area. He had Barbara beaten and tortured. When she refused to deny her new faith, her father asked the prefect for permission to put her to death. This he did by cutting off her head with an axe. She is patroness of firemen, mathematicians and carpenters.

Beatrice (*Latin:* Happiness)   July 29

Other Forms: Beatrix, Beatriz

Beatrice saw her two brothers martyred in Rome during the persecution of Diocletian (305), and when their bodies were thrown in the Tiber River she recovered them and buried them. She then went to live with St. Lucina, a Christian noblewoman. She was later arrested for being a Christian and was choked to death in prison.

Bernadette (Feminine of Bernard, *Greek:* Bold as a Bear)

Feb. 18

Other Forms: Bernardine, Bernice, Nadine

Bernadette was born in Lourdes, France, Jan. 7, 1844. Her family was very poor. One day (Feb. 11, 1858) she was out collecting sticks for firewood along the bank of the River Gave when a teenage girl appeared to her, dressed in a white robe with a blue sash and with a rosary in her hand. At first Bernadette did not know who she was and only gradually learned that she was Our Lady. She asked Bernadette to come back to the spot. Over the next year and a half she appeared eighteen times to the young French girl. She asked for prayers for sinners, for penance and that a chapel be built on the spot. When Bernadette asked the Lady who she was, she replied: "I am the Immaculate Conception." At first people did not believe Bernadette. She was made fun of and laughed at. Then pilgrims began to come to the spot of the visions. Church authorities and civil government at first opposed her. When the visions ended, Bernadette was sent to some Sisters in Nevers who cared for the sick and taught children. There Bernadette learned to read and write. Later she was permitted to join the convent there and became Sister Marie Bernard, working as infirmarian and sacristan. She was never strong and often ill. On April 16, 1879, she died, asking prayers because "I am a poor sinner." She was canonized by Pope Pius XI in 1933 and given the title "Lily of Mary." The great shrine of Lourdes which was built where Mary appeared to her has been a place of many miracles and cures of the sick.

Bertha (*Teutonic:* Strong One)

July 4

Other Forms: Berta, Bertild, Bertilla

St. Bertha was a holy English widow who built a monastery in northern France, where she governed as abbess. She died there about 725 A.D.

Brenda (*Teutonic:* Sword)

May 16

This is a feminine form for St. Brendan, a great Irish monk (May 16).

ST. BERNADETTE

Bridget (*Celtic:* Strength)

Other Forms: Birgit, Bride, Bridie, Bridig, Brigid, Brigida, Brigit, Brigitta, Brigitte

ST. BRIDGET (The Mary of Ireland)   (Feb. 1)

St. Bridget was born in Ireland about the middle of the 5th Century, of Christian parents who were said to have been baptized by St. Patrick himself. She is said to have been very holy as a child. She became a nun and founded the monastery of Kildare, the first house for Sisters in Ireland. She had great influence on the growth of the Church in Ireland and is reputed to have worked many miracles in her lifetime. She is called the second patron saint of Ireland, St. Patrick being the first. She died about 523 and was buried alongside St. Patrick. She is protectress of dairy workers.

ST. BRIDGET OF SWEDEN   (July 23)

St. Bridget of Sweden belonged to a noble family. She married Prince Ulf and had eight children, one of whom, Catherine, also became a saint. After the death of her husband she founded the Bridgettine Sisters. She had visions and revelations which she wrote down. Later she went to Rome to live and was the advisor to three popes. She died in Rome in 1373, shortly after returning from a pilgrimage to Jerusalem.

Camille (Feminine for Camillus,   July 14
Latin: Temple Servant)

Other Forms: Camelia, Camilla

St. Camillus de Lellis (July 14) was born in southern Italy in 1550 and died in Rome in 1614. He founded a religious order to care for the sick and is named the patron for the infirm.

Carmel (*Hebrew:* Orchard)   July 16

Other Forms: Carmelita, Carmella

A name given to the Blessed Virgin Mary, Our Lady of Mt. Carmel. Mount Carmel is associated with the Prophet Elijah and his defense of the faith of the people of Israel. In the Twelfth Century a group of hermits settled on the mountain and began the Carmelite Order, selecting as their patroness, Mary, Our Lady of Mt. Carmel.

Carol (Feminine for Charles, *Teutonic:* Strong)   Nov. 4

Other Forms: Arlene, Arlette, Carey, Carla, Carola, Carole, Caroline, Carolyn, Charlene, Charlotte, Cheryl

St. Charles Borromeo (Nov. 4) was made a bishop and cardinal at age 23. He became one of the great leaders in the Church of his time. Because of his service to the people during the Great Plague of 1576, the people called him a saint even before he died in 1584.

Catherine (*Greek:* Pure)   Apr. 29

Other Forms: Catalina, Caterina, Karen, Kate, Kateri, Katherine, Kathleen, Kathryn, Katrina, Kay, Kit, Kitty, Trina

St. Catherine of Siena, Virgin and Doctor (Teacher) of the Church, is one of the great figures of Christianity. Catherine was one of twin girls born to the Benincasa family of Siena, Italy, on March 23, 1347. She was a brilliant child who sought to imitate the child Jesus as closely as possible. When she was 18 she joined the Third Order of St. Dominic, and from then on lived a life of prayer and penance, which was blessed by her body having the stigmata (the wounds of Christ). Burning with the love of God, she worked for the poor and sick, and especially sought to bring sinners back to their religion. She labored to bring the popes back to Rome from Avignon. She had great influence on the affairs of the Church. Her writings still inspire those today who seek sanctity. She died in Rome, April 30, 1380, and was made a patroness of the city. Pope Pius XII made her protectress of nurses.

Other saints with this name:

St. Catherine of Sweden (Mar. 22), daughter of St. Bridget of Sweden. She was a holy nun who worked with her mother.

St. Catherine of Egypt (Nov. 29), a virgin, martyred for the faith in Alexandria, Egypt, 310 A.D.

St. Catherine Labouré, a French nun, who gave the world the Miraculous Medal and the prayer, "Oh, Mary, conceived without sin, pray for us who have recourse to you." She died in 1876 and her feast is Nov. 25.

ST. CATHERINE OF SIENA

Cecilia (*Latin:* Dim Sighted)

Nov. 22

Other Forms: Caecilia, Cecile, Cecily, Ceil, Cicely, Cicily, Sheila

St. Cecilia is one of the popular martyrs of the early Church who probably was put to death during one of the persecutions of the Second Century. Her remains were found in the catacombs and removed to a basilica built in Rome in her honor. She was born into a patrician family but was converted and became a zealous Christian. Cecilia was seized because she was a Christian and suffocated to death in her own house. She is the patroness of musicians.

Chantale (**For St. Jane Frances of Chantal [see],** *French:* Song)

Dec. 12

Charity (**English translation of** *Latin: Caritas*)

Aug. 1

Another Form: Cara (see: Faith)

Christina (**Feminine form of Christ,** *Greek*, Anointed)

July 24

Other Forms: Christiana, Christine, Kirsten, Kristin, Nina, Tina

St. Christina is a martyr of the early Church but the exact date is unknown. She lived in Rome and was converted there to Christianity. She had her father's idols of gold and silver melted down and gave the money to the poor. When her father learned of what she had done, he scourged her and turned her over to a judge who tortured her, trying to make her deny her faith. When she remained firm under torture she was put to death by archers.

Clare (*Latin:* Illustrious)   Aug. 11

Other Forms: Chiara, Claire, Clairette, Clara, Clareta, Clarice, Clarissa, Clarita

St. Clare was born into a prosperous family of Assisi, Italy, in 1193 or 1194. She grew up amid the luxuries and pleasures of the time, but she was not attached to them. Instead she learned with great interest that Francis Bernadone, also of Assisi, had given up the life of a playboy and had changed it to one of poverty in service of the poor. Some disciples had joined Francis at a chapel called the Portiuncula, and Clare was very impressed with their lives. Contrasting her own style of life with the poverty of the Franciscans, she could take no more. On Palm Sunday night, at age eighteen, she and her cousin Pacifica fled to the Portiuncula. Francis cut off their hair, had them dress in coarse brown wool, and received their religious vows. Thus were the Poor Clares or Franciscan Sisters born. Clare founded her convent at San Damiano, and it was soon crowded with Sisters, living the rule given them by Francis, which was one of poverty, living only on what they could beg each day. Francis called Clare "my little spiritual plant," and he directed her spiritual growth. For forty-two years she guided her Sisters, always a wise and loving mother. Once when marauding soldiers threatened to invade her convent, she met them at the door, carrying the monstrance with the Blessed Sacrament. They fled in shame. She survived St. Francis, dying in 1253. Her last words were: "Lord God, may you be blessed for having created me." Today her Sisters work all over the world, still serving the poor and needy.

Claudia (Feminine for Claude, *Latin:* Lame)   May 18

Other Forms: Claudette, Claudine

Claudia was a Christian woman who was arrested with six other women during the persecution of Galerius. When they refused to deny Jesus, they were forced to march naked to a lake, where they were drowned.

Clementine (Feminine for Clement,   Nov. 23
Latin: Merciful)

Other Forms: Clemence, Clementia, Clementina, Klementine

St. Clement was the third Pope after St. Peter and a first-century martyr. There are many other male saints by this name.

ST. CLARE OF ASSISI

Colette (Contracted form of Nicolette [see])   Mar. 6

Other Forms: Coleen, Colleen

St. Colette Boilet was born in France in 1380, the daughter of a carpenter. From the time she was a child she gave herself to prayer and serving the sick and the poor. She joined the Poor Clares, working to restore the early spirit of St. Francis and St. Clare. She had a particular devotion to Our Lord's Passion. She is reputed to have worked many miracles in her lifetime, one of them restoring a man to life. She died in Belgium in 1447.

Columbine (Feminine of Columban or Colman, *Latin-Gaelic:* Dove)

Other Forms: Colombina, Columba, Columbia, Columbina

There are many Irish saints, monks and missionaries of the sixth and seventh centuries whose name days could be used: St. Columba of Iona (June 9), St. Columbanus (Nov. 23), and several saints named Colman.

ST. COLUMBA OF SENS   (Dec. 31)

There is little information about this holy woman martyred in Gaul (ancient France).

Conception (From Immaculate Conception)   Dec. 8

Other Forms: Concepcion, Concepta

Many titles of the Blessed Virgin have been turned into popular names and given to a child as a sign of devotion to the Virgin Mary. Conception is such a name, being derived from Immaculate Conception, the name of a doctrine of the Church, defined in 1854, which teaches that Mary was born without original sin. It is also a title that Mary gave to herself during an appearance to Bernadette of Lourdes.

Constance (Feminine of Constantine, *Latin:* Firm) Jan. 28

Other Forms: Constantia, Constanza, Konstanze

Constance was the daughter of the Emperor Constantine. Before she was a Christian she went to pray at the tomb of St. Agnes that she might be cured of a disease that was taking her life. Her prayer was granted; she became a Christian, built a residence near the tomb, and spent the rest of her life there in prayer and good works.

Consuela (*Old Latin:* Consolation)

Other Forms: Consolata, Consuelo

This name is taken from another title of the Blessed Virgin: Our Lady of Consolation. Any feast day of Our Lady can be chosen as a patronal feast day but a good day is May 24, the Feast of Our Lady Help of Christians.

Cornelia (Feminine of Cornelius, *Latin:* Horn)

Another Form: Cora

Although this name is mainly from one of the men saints named Cornelius, such as St. Cornelius the Pope (Sept. 16) or St. Cornelius the Centurion (Feb. 2), there is a saint by this name listed in the Roman Martyrology as having been put to death in Africa along with other Christians, but nothing else is known of her. Her feast day is Mar. 31.

Cynthia (Feminine of Synesius, *Greek:* Understanding) Dec. 12

St. Synesius was a Roman martyr who was beheaded in 275 under the Emperor Aurelian. He is listed as having been in minor orders with the rank of lector (reader). His feast day is Dec. 12.

Daniela (Feminine of Daniel, *Hebrew:* The Lord is Judge)

Other Forms: Danielle, Danette

Daniel (July 21) was one of the four great prophets of the Old Testament. He wrote his book of Holy Scripture in Persia, where he died. St. Anthony Daniel (Oct. 19) is one of the North American martyrs put to death by the Iroquois Indians, July 4, 1648.

Daria (*Persian:* Preserver)   Oct. 25

Another Form: Darlene

Daria was a Persian woman, married to the Egyptian Chrysanthus. The couple lived in Rome where they were known for the zealous practice of the Christian Faith. Because of this they were arrested and put to death, A.D. 283.

Deborah (*Hebrew:* Bee)   Sept. 1

Other Forms: Debora, Debra

Deborah was a prophetess and judge among the Israelites who aided her people to overcome the Canaanites. She was a gifted woman, highly respected, a liberator of her people. The peace she brought about lasted forty years. Her story can be read in the fourth chapter of the Book of Judges, and the beautiful hymn she composed is in the fifth chapter.

Denise (Feminine form of Denis, *French* for Dionysius, *Greek:* God of Nyassa)   Oct. 9

St. Denis is the Patron of France. He was a missioner sent from Rome to preach the Gospel in Gaul, working in the area that now includes Paris, so he is considered the first bishop of that city. He and two companions were martyred there about the year 250. His feast is on Oct. 9.

Diana (*Latin:* Divine) June 9

Other Forms: Cynthia, Diane, Dinah

Blessed Diana of Andolo was a beautiful, sensitive girl of a good family in Bologna, Italy. She led a worldly life until one day she was converted by a sermon she heard at Mass. She immediately joined a convent but her family came and removed her by force. After two years, when her parents saw that she had not changed her mind, she was allowed to become a Dominican Sister. She died in 1236, age thirty-five.

Dolores (*Spanish:* Sorrows) Sept. 15

Other Forms: Dolor, Dolorita, Lola, Lolita

This is a name honoring the Blessed Virgin, Our Lady of Sorrows. When Mary brought Jesus to the Temple as an infant, she was met by Simeon who prophesied that she would suffer greatly. This she did in seeing her Son arrested, tortured and put to death. The Feast of Our Lady of Sorrows is September 15.

Dominica (Feminine for Dominic, *Latin:* I Belong to the Lord)

Other Forms: Dominga, Dominique

Although this name is usually given to honor the great St. Dominic Guzman, founder of the Dominican Order (feast Aug. 8), there is a Saint Dominica, virgin and martyr (feast July 6). She was a Christian maiden who was condemned to death under Diocletian for having destroyed pagan idols. The date is unknown.

Domitilla (Feminine of Domitian, May 12 *Latin:* Tame)

St. Domitilla was a martyr of first-century Rome, possibly a niece of the Emperor Domitian.

ST. DOROTHY

Donata (*Latin:* [God-] Given) Dec. 31

Other Forms: Dona, Donna, Donatilla

Donata was one of a group of Christian women put to death during an early Roman persecution. Her relics were found in the catacombs of Via Salaria along with the others. Nothing else is known about her.

Doris (**Feminine diminutive of Theodore,** Feb. 7
Greek: God's Gift)

Other Forms: Dora (see: Theodora), Doreen

Theodore (Feb. 7) was a soldier stationed with a Roman legion in the East. He was denounced as a Christian and released with a warning. Despite this, he set fire to a pagan temple. He was arrested and tortured, refusing to deny his faith. He was finally burned to death.

Dorothy (**Feminine of Theodore,** Feb. 6
Greek: God's Gift)

Other Forms: Dorothea (see: Theodora), Dorotea

St. Dorothy is a virgin and martyr who was scourged, racked and beheaded under the Emperor Diocletian (about 300 A.D.). While she was being questioned, one of her judges mocked her, telling her to send him roses and apples from the garden of the Heavenly Bridegroom of whom she spoke. On the day of her martyrdom, although it was winter, the flowers and fruit were mysteriously delivered to the judge. Her relics are kept in Rome.

Edith (*Old English:* Happiness) Sept. 16

Other Forms: Eadie, Eda, Edythe

St. Edith is an English saint, daughter of King Edgar. Her mother, St. Wilfrida (or Wulfridis), had become a nun in a monastery near Salisbury. She made her religious profession as a very young girl, and the

ST. ELIZABETH

Roman Martyrology in describing her says: "She did not leave the world; she never knew it." She spent her time caring for the poor and sick, especially for lepers. She died in 984 at the age of twenty-three.

Edwina (Feminine of Edwin, *Celtic:* Fire)   Oct. 12

Another Form: Edna

St. Edwin (Oct. 12) was the King of Northumbria (England). A pagan, he married a Christian bride and his wife's chaplain, St. Paulinus, converted him. From then on he worked for the conversion of his subjects. He died in battle in 633, fighting pagan Welshmen.

Eleanor (French Provincial for Helen [see])

Other Forms: Elenord, Eleonore, Elinor, Leanore, Lee, Lenora, Lenore, Leora, Nell, Nellie, Nelly

Most girls with this name are named after St. Helen (see). However, there was a St. Eleanore, martyred in Ireland in the 16th Century. Her feast is Dec. 29.

Elizabeth (*Hebrew:* God Has Sworn)

Other Forms: Alise, Aliza, Babette, Bella, Belle, Bess, Bessie, Beth, Betsy, Bette, Betty, Elisa, Elise, Eliza, Elsa, Else, Elsie, Isabel, Isabella, Isobel, Lee, Lilian, Lisa, Lisabeth, Lisbeth, Lise, Lisette, Lison

ST. ELIZABETH   (Nov. 5)

St. Elizabeth, wife of Zachary, was the cousin of the Blessed Virgin Mary and the mother of St. John the Baptist. All that we know of her comes from the first chapter of the Gospel of St. Luke. She was along in years when John was born. Some months earlier, Mary had come to visit her, having been told by the Angel Gabriel that Elizabeth was to become a mother. Of her son, Jesus said that no greater man had been born of woman.

ST. ELIZABETH OF HUNGARY

ST. ELIZABETH OF HUNGARY (Nov. 17)

St. Elizabeth of Hungary (1207-1231) was the daughter of the King of Hungary who was married to Louis, Duke of Thuringia, at the age of thirteen. She had four children, one son and three daughters. When her husband went on a crusade to the Holy Land and died there, she was driven from court by his wicked uncle. Forced to flee at night with a baby in her arms and her other children clinging to her, she took shelter in a pigsty. No one would help her for fear of the uncle. Finally, some Franciscans found her and took her and her children to shelter. Meanwhile her husband's soldiers returned from the crusade. Louis had made them promise that they would take care of his wife. She was recalled to court, the rights of her son restored. She joined the Third Order of Franciscans, founded a Franciscan convent, and died at the age of twenty-four.

ST. ELIZABETH OF PORTUGAL (July 4)

St. Elizabeth of Portugal was the daughter of the King of Aragon (Spain) and the great-niece of St. Elizabeth of Hungary. At the age of twelve she was married to Denis, King of Portugal. She was noted for her many charities to the poor, for her life of prayer, and for her efforts to make peace between Portugal and other kingdoms. After the death of her husband, she entered a Franciscan monastery (Poor Clares). She was born in 1271 and died in 1336 while on a journey to make peace between her son and grandson. Her last words were: "Mary, mother of grace."

ST. ELIZABETH ANN SETON (Jan. 4)

St. Elizabeth Ann Seton, first American-born saint of the United States, was an unusual woman. She was the mother of five children, a widow, a convert to Catholicism, and the foundress of an important teaching order (Sisters of Charity). St. Elizabeth was born in New York City on Aug. 28, 1774, just before the American Revolution began. Her family was socially prominent. When she was nineteen, she married William Seton. As a young wife and mother she engaged in the social activities of the time, going to the theater, attending Trinity (Episcopal) Church, and engaging in various charities. Her husband became seriously ill, and the Setons went to Italy in the hope that a change of climate would help him, but he died shortly after they reached Leghorn. The young widow was befriended by the Filicchi family, and the Catholic example these good people gave caused Mrs. Seton to look into the Catholic Church. When she returned to America with her children, she went to St. Peter's Church in New York and there became a Catholic. Because of this her friends abandoned her, her relatives attacked her, and her godmother disinherited her. The young widow was hard put to support her children. Conditions were so bad that she gladly accepted an invitation to go to Baltimore and open a Catholic school for girls. A year later (1809) she took the vows of a Sister and began the Sisters of Charity with four candidates. A piece of property at Emmitsburg, Maryland, was donated as a head-

ST. ELIZABETH ANN SETON

quarters. The first years were difficult, and often the Sisters did not have enough to eat. Despite the trials, the community grew, and when Mother Seton died at the age of forty-six on Jan. 4, 1821, it was well established. Pope Paul VI added her name to the Church's list of saints.

Emily (Feminine of Emil, *Latin:* Excelling)

Other Forms: Amelia, Emelie, Emeline, Emilia, Emiliana, Emma

ST. EMMA (Apr. 19)

Emma was the wife of a Count Ludger in what is now Germany. After her husband died, she spent the next forty years along with her fortune in the works of the Church. She aided the poor, built churches, and tended the sick. She died about 1050.

BL. EMILY BICCIERE (May 3)

Blessed Emily (1238-1314) was born into a wealthy Italian family of Vercelli. She had her father build a convent, and there when she was eighteen she returned with some friends. They lived as religious under the rule of St. Dominic.

Enrica (Feminine of Henry, *Teutonic:* Home Ruler) July 15

Another Form: Henrietta (see: Harriet)

St. Henry (July 15) was emperor of the Holy Roman Empire who was called "the most Christian prince" because of his own goodness and his work to spread the Church. He died in 1024.

Erica (Feminine of Eric, *Norse:* Ever-Ruler) May 18

Another Form: Erika

St. Eric (May 18) was King of Sweden who led a holy life. He died in battle in 1160 or 1161.

Ernestine (Feminine of Ernest)   Nov. 7

St. Ernest was a German baron who took part in the second crusade. He was captured by the Moslems and, refusing to embrace their religion, died a frightful death of martyrdom in 1148. His feast is Nov. 7.

Esperanza (*Spanish:* Hope)   Aug. 1

See: Faith.

Esther (*Persian:* Star)   July 1

Other Forms: Edissa, Vanessa

Esther was one of the great women of the Old Testament. There is a book of the Bible named after her which recounts her many deeds in behalf of the people of Israel.

Etheldra (*Old English:* Noble Maiden)   June 23

Other Forms: Audrey, Ethel, Etheldreda, Ethelreda

St. Etheldra was the daughter of the King of East Anglia and the wife of the King of Northumbria. Thus this English woman was both princess and queen. After twelve years of marriage she entered the convent and was chosen abbess of a monastery on the Isle of Ely. Her holy life attracted many to her. She died June 23, 679.

Eugenia (Feminine of Eugene,   Dec. 25
Greek: Well Born)

Other Forms: Eugenie, Gina

St. Eugenia is honored by the Church as a virgin and martyr. She was a wealthy young woman of Rome who was converted by two of her slaves,

Saints Protus and Hyacinth. She was said to have been well educated. She was arrested during the persecution of Valerian along with the two slaves who had converted her. She was put to death in her prison on Christmas Day, 257.

Eulalia (*Greek:* Fair-spoken) Dec. 10

Another Form: Eulalie

A popular saint of Spain. Her devotion was brought to the New World by Spanish colonists. She was a Christian maiden who was arrested during the persecution of Diocletian. After suffering many tortures, she was burned at the stake in 304. A white dove is said to have appeared over her as she died and also later over her ashes, which were gathered up and are preserved in Oviedo, Spain.

Eunice (*Greek:* Happy Victory) Dec. 23

This is a feminine form for St. Eunician (Eunicianus), whose feast is celebrated on Dec. 23. He was one of a group of Christians martyred on the island of Crete during the persecution of the Emperor Decian (A.D. 250). He was beheaded, and his relics were later moved to Rome.

Eve (*Hebrew:* Life) Sept. 6

Other Forms: Eva, Eveline, Evelyn, Evita

St. Eve is the patroness of the city of Dreux, France, where her relics are kept and she is honored as a martyr.

Fabiola (Feminine of Fabina, *Latin:* Artisan) Dec. 27

St. Fabiola was a wealthy woman of fourth-century Rome who reformed her life and became a friend of St. Jerome.

ST. FRANCES XAVIER CABRINI

Faith (English translation of *Latin: Fides*)   Aug. 1

Other Forms: Fay, Fe, Fidelia

St. Faith, the legend goes, was one of the three daughters of St. Sophia (Wisdom), who lived in Rome in the second century. St. Sophia named her daughters after the three great virtues — Faith, Hope, and Charity — and taught them to be good Christians. They were all arrested during the persecution of the Emperor Hadrian and, after being tortured in an effort to get them to deny Christ, were put to death when they refused to give up their faith. St. Faith was then twelve years old.

ST. FAITH OF AGEN   (Oct. 6)

This St. Faith is said to have been martyred on a gridiron in third-century Gaul (France). She is much revered in England.

Felicia (Diminutive of Felicitas, *Latin:* Happy)   Nov. 23

Other Forms: Felice, Felicienne, Felicita, Felicitas, Felicity

St. Felicity was one of the most popular saints in the early Church. She was a holy widow with seven sons. The family was arrested about 165 A.D. and brought before the Emperor Antoninus Pius. She encouraged her boys to remain firm and was forced to watch them die one by one. Five months later, on November 23, she herself was beheaded, having refused to deny Christ.

ST. FELICITY OF AFRICA   (Mar. 7)

Saint Felicity is listed in the universal calendar of the Church with her feast on March 7. She was arrested in Carthage (Africa) along with St. Perpetua in the year 203. She was not yet a Christian but was baptized immediately after her arrest. She was with child at the time. A daughter was born to her three days before she was to die. She gave the child to a Christian woman. When she was brought into the amphitheater, wild beasts mauled her but did not kill her. A gladiator was finally sent to end her life with a blow to the head. Another gladiator strangled St. Perpetua.

Felipa (Spanish feminine of Philip, *Greek:* Lover of Horses)

St. Philip (May 3) was one of the Twelve Apostles.

Florence (*Latin:* Flowering)

Other Forms: Fleur, Flora, Florentia, Florentina

Florence was originally a male name, and there are many male saints with this name. Two female saints are:

ST. FLORENTINE (FLORENCE)   (June 20)

St. Florence was the sister of the famous St. Isidore of Seville. She was born in Cartagena, Spain, and was left an orphan at an early age, to be raised by another brother, St. Leander. She entered a convent, where she became an abbess. She died in great holiness about 640 A.D.

ST. FLORA (FLORENCE)   (Nov. 24)

St. Flora was a Christian girl who was arrested with another girl, Maria, during a Moslem persecution in Cordova, Spain. The two girls had a long imprisonment before being executed in 856.

Frances (Feminine of Francis, *Teutonic:* Free)

Other Forms: Cesca, Fanchon, Fanny, Fenna, France, Francesca, Franchette, Francine, Francoise, Frannie

This name is usually given in honor of St. Francis of Assisi (Oct. 4). However, there are two well-known women saints with this name.

ST. FRANCES XAVIER CABRINI   (Nov. 13)

St. Frances Xavier Cabrini is an American saint. Although she was born in Italy, when she came to America she became a citizen of the United States, and thus was the first American to be declared a saint. Mother Cabrini founded a community of sisters and came to the United States in order to take care of Italian immigrants. She became a familiar figure on the lower East Side of New York as she walked the streets searching for the poor she could help. Later her work took her to Chicago where as in New York she founded a large hospital. She died in Chicago on Dec. 22, 1915, and is buried in New York. She became a saint on July 7, 1946.

ST. FRANCES OF ROME

St. Frances was married at the age of twelve and had three children, a son and two daughters. Pious by nature, she became a model wife and mother. "A wife must find God in her household work," she said. She found time to visit the sick in hospitals and aid the poor. When after forty years of married life her husband died, Frances entered the Oblates of Mary, which she had founded years earlier. Here she spent the last four years of her life doing penance and works of piety. She died March 9, 1440.

Freda (From Alfreda, feminine of Alfred, *Teutonic:* Good Counsellor)

May 20

Other Forms: Alfreda, Alfrida, Althryda

St. Alfreda was the daughter of King Offa of Mercia in Britain. She was betrothed to King Ethelbert of East Anglia who was treacherously murdered by her father. After her husband-to-be's death in 792, she fled the court and lived the rest of her life as a hermit. She died in 834.

Frederica (Feminine of Frederic, *Teutonic*: Peace-Ruler)

Another Form: Frederika

There were several saints named Frederick. One of them was the grandson of the King of the Frisians who became bishop of Utrecht (Holland) in 820. He labored to end paganism in the country, thus making enemies. He was stabbed to death at the end of Mass, July 18, 838 (also his feast date).

Gabriela (Feminine of Gabriel, *Hebrew:* God's Strength)

Sept. 29

Other Forms: Gabriella, Gabrielle, Briel

St. Gabriel, the Archangel, is one of the three angels mentioned by name in the Bible. He appeared twice to the Prophet Daniel to explain a

ST. GENEVIEVE

46

vision concerning the Messiah. In the New Testament, Gabriel appears first to the priest Zechariah to announce that his wife will give birth to a son who is to be called John (John the Baptist). He identified himself as "Gabriel, who stands in the presence of God." Six months later he appeared to the Virgin Mary to announce that she was to become the mother of Jesus. St. Luke tells the story in the first chapter of his Gospel.

Gemma (*Italian:* Jewel) Apr. 11

St. Gemma Galgani (1878-1903) was a child in a poor family in Tuscany, Italy. Although afflicted with many sufferings, she had complete trust in God. As a result she was given great graces and heavenly revelations.

Genevieve (*Celtic:* White Wave) Jan. 3

Other Forms: Ginette, Violane, Yolanda, Blanche

St. Genevieve is the patroness of Paris, France. She was born just outside the city in 422, and when she was seven years old she met St. Germanus, who foretold that she would be a saint and do great things. At the age of fifteen, she took a vow of virginity and accepted the veil of the Spouses of Christ. She is said to have had the gift of being able to read consciences and then advising people about their lives. When the Franks besieged Paris, St. Genevieve devised a plan to feed the city and thus saved it. Again when Attila the Hun was marching on Paris, St. Genevieve kept the people from fleeing by promising that Attila would never enter Paris. When the invader turned his army and bypassed Paris, marching towards Orleans, where he was defeated by the Romans and Franks, the people of Paris attributed their salvation to her prayers. She died in 512 and the church where she was buried was given her name. Her relics were lost in the anti-Catholic French Revolution and her great church was renamed the Pantheon.

Georgia (Feminine of George, *Greek:* Farmer)

Other Forms: Georgianna, Georgana, Georgette

This name is usually given for St. George, patron saint of England. He suffered martyrdom in Palestine in 303. His feast is Apr. 23.

St. Georgia is a virgin who lived in Auvergne (France) about 500 A.D. She dwelt in a countryside hermitage where she fasted and prayed all day. Many miracles have been attributed to her. At her death a flock of white doves is said to have appeared. They accompanied her body to the church and then to the cemetery, leaving only after her burial.

Geraldine (Feminine of Gerald, *Teutonic:* Spear Ruler)

Other Forms: Geralda, Geralyn

St. Gerald (Mar. 13) was an Irish monk who became Abbot of Mayo. He led a very holy life, given to much prayer and fasting. He died about 722.

Germaine (Feminine of Germain, *Teutonic:* Kin)

June 15

St. Germaine Cousin was a poor crippled girl who was born near Toulouse, France, in 1579. Her mother died when she was an infant, and her father had little love for her. When he remarried, her stepmother persecuted her, forcing her to sleep under a stairway in the barn. Every day she had to take the sheep to pasture and guard them. Because she could not read or write, she used her rosary for prayer. Each day she went to Mass, leaving her sheep in God's care, and He certainly watched over them, because she never lost a sheep despite the fact that there were many wolves in the area. She was only given dry bread to eat, and she often shared this with some poor person. One day in 1601 when she was twenty-two, her father noticed that the sheep had not been taken to pasture. He went to the barn and found Germaine dead on her bed of twigs beneath the stairs. Forty years later when her coffin was opened as the first step towards her canonization as a saint, it was discovered that her body had not decayed. Many miracles have been attributed to this abused crippled girl who loved God so greatly despite her hard life.

48

ST. GERMAINE

49

Gertrude (*Teutonic:* Spear Strength) — Nov. 16

Other Forms: Gerda, Trudy

St. Gertrude was a German girl who entered a convent of Cistercian Sisters, where she became noted for her scholarship and intelligence. She gave herself to study, particularly in philosophy. One day she had a vision in which Our Lord appeared to her and rebuked her for neglecting Him for her studies. From then on the only books she used were the Bible and the writings of the Fathers of the Church. She then became known for her prayer and contemplation. She died in 1301.

Gladys (*Cymric:* Delicate) — Mar. 29

St. Gladys was a saint of the Fifth Century. She was the daughter of a famous Welsh chieftain, wife of St. Gundleus and mother of St. Cadoc.

Gloria (*Latin:* Glory)

A name referring to the glory or splendor of God. There are no saints with this name in the Roman calendar.

Grace (**From the Latin:** *Gratia*) — July 5

St. Grace is a Cornish (English) saint who was married to St. Probus. Nothing else is known about her and her husband except that they are the patron saints of the parish church in Tresilian.

Guadalupe (**Spanish rendition of Coatlaxupeuh,** *Aztec:* My Image Will Crush the Serpent God) — Dec. 12

Other Forms: Guadaloupe, Lupe

The name Guadalupe is that given to the oldest shrine to the Blessed Virgin Mary in the Americas. It is also used as a name to honor the appearance of the Blessed Virgin Mary there. In early December, 1531, an

Indian convert, Juan Diego, was crossing Tepeyac hill near Mexico City when he met a beautiful woman, who told him to go and tell the bishop that she wanted a church built there where people could come and pray. Juan delivered the message, but the bishop did not believe him. On December 12, Juan was crossing the hill again, and again he met the Lady. Although it was winter, she told him to pick some roses growing nearby and take them to his bishop. Juan gathered up the roses in his cloak and carried them to the bishop. When he opened the cloak the roses fell out, and on the cloak was a picture of the Lady as Juan had described her. The bishop believed, and the church to Our Lady was built and has become one of the world's greatest shrines. The famous picture is enshrined in this basilica, and scientists who have examined it cannot say how it was made or why it has never faded or why the rough fabric has not decayed. Various popes have honored the Shrine of Our Lady of Guadalupe, and Mary under this title is named Queen of Mexico and Empress of the Americas.

Gwen (*Welsh:* White) July 5

Another Form: Gwendoline

St. Gwen was a refugee from Britain (fifth century) who fled to Brittany (France) in the upheaval following the withdrawal of the Romans. There is a church in Brittany still dedicated to her.

ST. GWENDOLINE (Mar. 28)

St. Gwendoline was a holy nun in Alsace. She was raised by her aunt, St. Odilla, whom she succeeded as abbess. She died about 750 A.D.

Harriet (Dimunitive feminine of Henry, July 15
Teutonic: Home Ruler)

Other Forms: Hally, Harietta, Harriette, Henrietta, Henriette

St. Henry was a German emperor born in 973. He was given the title "Most Christian Prince" because of his efforts in behalf of religion. He sponsored missioners, founded churches and monasteries and protected the pope. He also lived the Christian virtues.

Helen (*Greek:* Light) Aug. 18

Other Forms: Aileen, Alene, Aline, Celine, Eileen, Elain, Elaine, Elane, Eleanore, Elena, Ella, Ellen, Helena, Helene, Ilona, Lena, Lenore, Nell, Nellie, Selina, Seline

St. Helena was the wife of Constantius Chlorus and the mother of Constantine, the first Christian Emperor of Rome. It was Constantine who converted his mother to his new religion, and from that time on she became fervent in her faith, building churches and aiding the poor. About 325 A.D. she made a pilgrimage to the Holy Land and had excavations made of sites connected with Jesus. In one of those excavations near Calvary, the cross on which Jesus died was discovered. She had basilicas built at Bethlehem and on the Mount of Olives. She died about 328.

Hilda (*Old English:* Battle Maiden) Nov. 17

Another Form: Hildegarde

St. Hilda was a Northumbrian (English) princess who had been baptized by St. Paulinus. She entered a convent in Yorkshire over which she became abbess. Noted for her wisdom, her counsel was sought by people from all walks of life, even public officials. She died in 680 after a long and painful illness.

ST. HILDEGARDE (Sept. 17)

St. Hildegarde was born in Germany in 1098 and became a nun there. She was gifted with the spirit of prophecy and wrote a book of Revelations. She later became abbess of her monastery, dying in 1179.

Hope (**English translation of Latin:** *Spes*) Aug. 1

See: Faith

ST. HELENA

53

Ida (*Greek:* Happy) Apr. 3

St. Ida was a French noblewoman, daughter of the Duke of Lorraine, who married the Count of Boulogne, and whose daughter became Empress of Germany. Despite her wealth and position, she was known for her humility and charity. She had St. Anselm for her spiritual director. After the death of her husband, she used her wealth to establish religious houses. She died in 1113.

Ignatia (Feminine of Ignatius, *Greek:* Fiery) July 31

St. Ignatius Loyola (1491-1556) was the founder of the Jesuit Order.

Immaculata (*Latin:* Spotless) Dec. 8

This is a name given in honor of Our Lady of the Immaculate Conception, patroness of the United States under this title.

Irene (*Greek:* Peace)

Other Forms: Irena, Renata, Renée

ST. IRENE, VIRGIN AND MARTYR (Apr. 5)

St. Irene was the Sister of Sts. Agape and Chionia, who with them was burned at the stake in Greece during the persecution of Diocletian (304 A.D.).

ST. IRENE OF PORTUGAL (Oct. 20)

St. Irene was a Portuguese nun who died defending her virtue in 653. Her body was thrown into the Tagus River and recovered. She was canonized because of the many miracles that occurred at her grave. Her shrine is at Santarem (Saint Irene) which takes its name from the martyr.

Irma (*Teutonic:* Strong) Dec. 24

Other Forms: Erma, Irmina, Irmine

St. Irma was a princess, the daughter of King Dagobert of Austrasia, she was engaged to be married to a Merovingian prince who died before the wedding could take place. St. Irma then founded a convent which she entered. She lived a very holy life and is noted for her charities. She died about 710 A.D.

Jacqueline (Diminutive of Jacques, French for James [Jacob], *Hebrew:* Supplanter) Feb. 8

Another Form: Jacoba

Blessed Jacqueline, a member of the Roman nobility, was a close friend of both St. Clare and St. Francis of Assisi. Although she became a widow, she could not enter the religious life of St. Clare because she had to raise two sons. Because of her energy in behalf of the new religious order, St. Francis called her "Brother Jacoba." When Francis lay dying, he sent for Jacqueline, telling her to bring the things necessary for his burial. She spent her last years in Assisi and is buried close to St. Francis.

(This name is also given for St. James, the name of two of Our Lord's Apostles, honored May 3 and July 25.)

Jane (Feminine of John, *Hebrew:* God Has Mercy)

Other Forms: Giovanna, Janet, Janice, Jean, Jeanette, Jeanine, Jeanne, Jessica, Jessie, Joan, Jo Ann, Joanna, Joanne, Johanna, Juana, Juanita, June, Nita

This name is usually given in honor of one of the saints named John, of whom there are many. It is usually in honor of St. John the Apostle and Evangelist, friend of Our Lord (Dec. 27), or of John the Baptist (June 24, Aug. 29).

ST. JOAN OF ARC

ST. JANE CHANTAL   (Dec. 12)

St. Jane Frances, Baroness of Chantal, was born in France in 1572. At twenty she married the Baron de Chantal and had eight happy years of married life before he was killed in a hunting accident. She then spent her time caring for her children and aiding the poor and sick. The turning point in her life came when she met St. Francis de Sales in the house of her father. St. Francis became her confessor and spiritual director. In 1610 under the guidance of St. Francis she founded the Sisters of the Visitation, who spread rapidly in Europe and came to Canada with the early settlers. Her last years were ones of physical suffering. She died Dec. 15, 1643. Both she and St. Francis are buried together at the Visitation Motherhouse in Savoy.

ST. JOAN OF ARC   (May 30)

St. Joan of Arc is the heroine of France. She is also known as Maid of Orleans. Joan was born in Domrémy, Jan. 6, 1410. Her country at the time was largely in the power of the English. As a girl she cared for the sheep in the fields and from the age of thirteen began to hear voices, which she said were those of St. Michael, St. Catherine and St. Margaret. In 1428 her voices told Joan to go find the King of France and help him reconquer his country. She saw the Dauphin, rallied an army behind her, and marched on Orleans while the English fled. One by one she freed the cities of France: Tours, Beaugency, Patay, Troyes, Soissons, Château-Thierry, Crécy, Provins, and so on. She was present at Rheims when the Dauphin was crowned king, July 17, 1429. She continued to lead her army until she was betrayed by the Duke of Burgundy, who took her prisoner and sold her to the Bishop of Beauvais, a servant of the English, for 10,000 gold francs. The bishop put her on trial for treason and heresy, and his court condemned her to be burned at the stake. She was treated most shamefully and was denied the Blessed Sacrament before she died, May 30, 1431. Some years later at the request of her mother and brothers, the trial was reviewed and the verdict reversed. The Church approved of her life by beatifying her and then canonizing her in 1920.

Jennifer (Feminine of Wilfred,   Oct. 12
            Old English: Firm Peace)

St. Wilfred was one of the great bishops of the Anglo-Saxon Church. He became Archbishop of York and more than once was banished from England. He spent his period of exile doing missionary work in such places as Sussex, the Isle of Wight and Holland. He founded many monasteries. He died Apr. 24, 709.

(Sometimes this name is taken as a form of Jane or Genevieve [see]).

Josephine (Feminine of Joseph, *Hebrew:* Increase) Mar. 19

Other Forms: Giuseppina, Josefa, Josepha, Josette, Josianne, Yvette

This name is given in honor of St. Joseph, foster father of Our Lord and husband of Mary.

Judith (Feminine of Jude, *Hebrew:* Praised) Oct. 28

Another Form: Judy

This name is given in honor of St. Jude Thaddeus, an Apostle and relative of Our Lord. According to tradition, he preached the Gospel in Persia and died there. He is the patron for desperate cases.

Julia (*Latin:* Downy) May 22

Other Forms: Jill, Juliana, Julianna, Julie, Juliet, Juliette

St. Julia was a noble maiden who lived in Carthage in North Africa. In 439 Genseric the Vandal besieged and sacked the city, taking prisoners, among whom was Julia. She was sold as a slave to a pagan merchant of Syria. Later she was with her master on a business voyage when the boat was shipwrecked off Corsica. She was captured by pagans and when she refused to honor idols was crucified. Her body was later moved to Leghorn, Italy, of which city she is the patroness.

Other saints with this name:

Julie Billiart *April 8*
Juliana Falconiere *June 19*
Julia of Portugal *Oct. 1*
Julia of Troyes *July 21*
Juliana, Martyr *Feb. 16*

Justina (*Latin:* Just)   Sept. 26

Other Forms: Justa, Justine, Tina

St. Justa was a tradeswoman in Seville, Spain, poor but holy. She was arrested for her religion at the outbreak of the persecution of Diocletian (287). She was tortured by stretching on the rack. She died as the result while still in prison. She is greatly honored in Spain.

Laura (Feminine of Lawrence, *Latin:* Laurel)   Oct. 19

Other Forms: Lara, Laraine, Laureen, Laurenta, Laurentia, Laurette, Loretta, Lorraine

St. Laura was a married woman who after the death of her husband entered the convent of St. Mary of Culédor in Spain, where she became abbess. She was arrested by the Saracens and thrown into a great vat of boiling tar. The date is unknown.

ST. LAURENTIA   (Oct. 8)

St. Laurentia was a slave who converted her mistress, Palatias, to Christianity. Both women were arrested during the persecution of Diocletian (302) and put to death. Their relics are honored at Fermo, Italy.

Leona (Feminine of Leo, *Latin:* Lion)

Other Forms: Lee, Leonie, Leonita

St. Leo the Great (Nov. 10) was one of the most outstanding popes of the Catholic Church. He died in 461.

Lilian (*Latin:* Lily)

Other Forms: Lila, Lily, Lillian

This name is given in honor of the Blessed Virgin, whose symbol is a white lily, denoting her purity. Any feast of the Blessed Virgin can be selected as a personal feast day, although Dec. 8 would be very appropriate.

Louise (Feminine of Louis, *Teutonic:* Famous Warrior)

Mar. 15

Other Forms: Alison, Aloysia, Eloisa, Eloise, Héloïse, Lois, Louisa, Luisa, Luise

St. Louise de Marillac was born in Paris in 1591. Her mother died when she was a child, and she early had to learn the management of her father's household. She married, and after nine years her husband became an invalid. She nursed him for the next four years. After his death she went to see her friend and counselor, St. Vincent de Paul. She told him that she would like to become a nun. St. Vincent replied that he was looking for someone to begin a sisterhood similar to his congregation for men. Together they founded the Sisters of Charity, of which St. Louise became superior general. As the Sisters grew in number they began works of education, hospitals for the poor, homes for abandoned children, and an apostolate to the galley slaves. In 1660 when she lay dying she sent word to St. Vincent. He was seriously ill himself and could not come to her, but he sent a message which said, "You go on ahead and I hope to see you soon in heaven." She died on Mar. 15 of that year.

(If this name is given in honor of St. Louis, King of France, his feast is celebrated Aug. 25.)

Lucy (Feminine of Luke, *Greek:* Light)

Dec. 13

Other Forms: Luc, Luce, Lucette, Lucia, Lucie, Lucien, Lucienne, Lucilla, Lucille, Lucina, Lucinda, Luz

St. Lucy is a popular martyr of the early Church whose name is recorded in the First Eucharistic Prayer of the Mass. She is patroness for people with eye diseases. She was born in Syracuse, a great city of Sicily. Her mother had her engaged to a young man, but she put off marrying him for three years because she had vowed her virginity to Jesus. One day she went to the tomb of St. Agnes to pray for the conversion of her mother, and as she returned home, she was arrested. The persecution of Diocletian was then raging. She had been betrayed as a Christian by the young man to whom she had been engaged. She was taken before the judges but refused to deny her faith. She was sentenced to be burned, but as the fire died down she was still alive, so a soldier pierced her throat with his sword. She died in 304, prophesying that peace would soon come to the Church (which it did under the Emperor Constantine).

(The Feast of St. Luke the Evangelist is Oct. 18.)

ST. LUCY

Lydia (From Ludia, *Greek:* An area of Asia Minor) Aug. 3

St. Lydia was the first convert made by St. Paul in Europe. She lived in an area of Macedonia that was famous for its purple-dyed cloth, and she made her living selling this cloth. St. Paul met her on the bank of a river with some other women to whom he explained Christianity. Lydia became a convert and was baptized with her household. She invited St. Paul to stay at her house, which he did. Her story is in the Acts of the Apostles.

Mabel (*Latin:* Lovable)

Mabel is a diminutive from Amabilis, a term taken from the Litany of the Blessed Virgin Mary. Any feast day of Mary can be used as a name day.

Magdalene (*Hebrew:* Person from Magdala) July 22

Other Forms: Maddalena, Madeline, Magda, Marlene

St. Mary Magdalene was a disciple and close friend of Jesus. According to the Gospels she was at one time a great sinner, but after meeting Jesus she became a great saint. Many believe she is the same Mary who later lived in Bethany, near Jerusalem, with her sister, Martha, and her brother, Lazarus. Jesus frequently went to her house, and it was there that he raised Lazarus from the dead. She was present at the Crucifixion and she was the first one Jesus appeared to after the Resurrection. There are two traditions about Mary. One of the Eastern Church says she went to Ephesus to live with the Blessed Virgin and St. John. That of the Western Church says that with Martha and Lazarus she went to France to preach the Gospel.

Manuela (Feminine diminutive of Emmanuel, *Hebrew:* God With Us)

Emmanuel is a name given to the Messiah by the Prophet Isaiah. Any feast of Jesus can celebrate this day but the most appropriate day is Christmas, Dec. 25, which commemorates the day that God came among us.

ST. MARY MAGDALENE

Marcella (Feminine of Marcellus, Latin: Of Mars)

Jan. 31

Other Forms: Marcelina, Marcelle

Marcella was a wealthy patrician woman of Rome. She lost her husband after seven months of marriage and refused to marry again. Although she lived in the world, she tried to follow the Gospel precepts after the fashion of Egyptian hermits. She had been introduced to this life by St. Athanasius, who at that time was in exile in Rome. She was also a close friend of St. Jerome, who taught her Scripture and who called her "a model of widowhood and sanctity." Marcella was in Rome when Alaric's Goths sacked the city. She was beaten to make her reveal where her riches were, goods long before given to the poor. She died a few days afterwards (in 410).

Marcia (Feminine form of Mark, Latin: Of Mars)

Apr. 25

Another Form: Marsha

Although there were several martyrs in the early Church with the name of Marcia, which was popular among Roman women, the name is usually given for St. Mark the Evangelist, whose feast is Apr. 25.

Margaret (Greek: Pearl)

July 20

Other Forms: Greta, Gretchen, Madge, Maggie, Maisie, Margarita, Marge, Margery, Margo, Margot, Marguerite, Marina, Marjorie, Pearl, Pegeen, Peggy, Rita

St. Margaret, who is invoked by those with kidney disease and women in childbirth, is a popular saint in the Greek Church, and her devotion spread in the West after the Crusades. She was born in Asia Minor, where her father was a pagan priest. She was converted by a servant and vowed to remain a virgin out of love for Christ. When her father learned of her religion, he drove her from his house, and she had to become a shepherdess. She was arrested and put to death by the sword. She lived in the third century.

ST. MARGARET OF SCOTLAND

ST. MARGARET OF SCOTLAND (Nov. 10)

Margaret was related to St. Stephen, King of Hungary. She married Malcolm III, King of Scotland. She is known for her good works in behalf of religion and the oppressed. She died at Edinburgh in 1093.

ST. MARGARET MARY ALACOQUE (Oct. 10)

St. Margaret Mary was born in France in 1647. She joined the Visitation Sisters at Paray-le-Monial and advanced rapidly in spiritual perfection. As a result of revelations made to her by Our Lord, she promoted devotion to the Sacred Heart, despite much opposition. Today that devotion has spread worldwide. She died in 1690.

Martha *(Aramaic:* Lady) July 29

Other Forms: Marta, Marthe

St. Martha was the sister of Mary of Bethany (who may have been formerly Mary Magdalene) and Lazarus. She was a friend of Jesus, and it was at her request that Jesus raised Lazarus from the dead. She entertained Jesus in her home and took care of His needs. She is the patroness of innkeepers and restaurant owners. According to Western tradition, she along with Mary and Lazarus went to France to spread the Gospel after the Resurrection of Jesus.

Martina (Feminine of Martin, *Latin:* Warlike) Jan. 1

Another Form: Martine

Martina was a Roman girl who was arrested at prayer during the reign of Alexander Severus (third century). She was tortured but refused to deny Christ. She was beheaded near Ostia and her body brought back to Rome where a church was built in her honor.

ST. MARTHA

Mary (*Hebrew:* Rebellion)

Other Forms: Mae, Maime, Mara, Maria, Marian, Marianna, Maribel, Marie, Marietta, Mariette, Marigold, Marilyn, Marya, Maureen, May, Mirelle, Miriam, Moira, Molly, Polly

Mary is the most celebrated of all women because she was the mother of Jesus Christ, the Son of God. Her most popular title is The Blessed Virgin. It is the teaching of the Church to which all Catholics must give consent that Mary was conceived without being touched by original sin. She was the daughter of Ann and Joachim, who lived in Nazareth. She was engaged to a carpenter in Nazareth named Joseph. The Gospels tell how the Angel Gabriel told her that she was to have a son who should be named Jesus, who would be born to her by the power of the Holy Spirit. With Joseph she went to Bethlehem to be enrolled in a census which the Roman emperor had ordered. There Jesus was born in a manger. Later she and Joseph and the Child fled to Egypt to escape Herod the King, who ordered all babies in Bethlehem to be killed because the Magi had told him that one of them would be King of the Jews. After Herod died, Mary, Joseph, and the Child returned to Nazareth where Jesus grew up. Mary followed Jesus during His preaching and was beneath the Cross when He died. From the Cross Jesus gave her to the care of His Apostle John. She was present in the Upper Room at the descent of the Holy Spirit on Pentecost Day. Tradition says she and John went to Ephesus to live and it was from there that she was assumed into heaven.

There are many feasts honoring the Blessed Virgin under various titles, and any one of these can be chosen as a personal feast day for those named in honor of Mary. Some of these are:

Mary, Mother of God (*Jan. 1*)
Birthday of Mary (*Sept. 8*)
Assumption of Mary (*Aug. 15*)
Immaculate Conception (*Dec. 8*) — See Conception
Our Lady of Lourdes (*Feb. 11*)
Our Lady of Mt. Carmel (*July 16*) — See Carmel
Our Lady of Ransom (*Sept. 24*)
Our Lady of the Rosary (*Oct. 7*) — See Rosaria
Our Lady of Sorrows (*Sept. 15*) — See Dolores
Presentation of Mary (*Aug. 22*)
Visitation of Mary (*May 31*)
Our Lady of Mercy (*Sept. 24*) — See Mercedes
Our Lady of the Snows (*Aug. 5*)
Holy Name of Mary (*Sept. 12*)

Some other saints with this name:

St. Maria Goretti (July 5)
St. Mary Magdalene (July 22) — See Magdalene
St. Mary Magdalene of Pazzi (May 25)
St. Mary of Egypt (Apr. 22)

BLESSED VIRGIN MARY

Matilda (*Teutonic:* Battle Maiden)   Mar. 14

Other Forms: Mathilde, Maud, Maude, Tilda, Tillie

Matilda, a descendant of Saxon kings, was married to the German emperor Henry the Fowler. One of her sons, Otto, became the Emperor of Germany, and another son, Henry, was Duke of Bavaria. After the death of her husband, these two sons deprived their mother of all her possessions, and she had to take shelter in a convent. There she lived a life of holiness and poverty. Later Otto's wife and some German bishops persuaded her sons to give her back her possessions, which she then used to build hospitals and churches. She founded two famous German monasteries. She died in 968.

Maura (Feminine of Maurice, *Greek:* Dark)   Nov. 30

St. Maura was a Christian martyr who died in Constantinople but the date and manner of her death have been lost. An island in the Mediterranean Sea is named after her.

Melanie (*Greek:* Dark)   Dec. 31

Other Forms: Melania, Melinda

St. Melanie and her husband, Oinianus, were a wealthy and prominent Roman couple. Among their friends were Sts. Jerome and Augustine. After their two children died, they gave their wealth to the poor and went to the Holy Land, where they lived in a monastery they had founded. She died in 439.

Mercedes (From Merced, *Spanish:* Mercy)   Sept. 24

Other Forms: Merced, Mercy

A name given in honor of the Blessed Virgin who has as one of her titles for which there is a Mass and feast, Our Lady of Mercy. See: Mary.

Michaela (Feminine of Michael,
Hebrew: Who Is Like God?)

Sept. 29

Other Forms: Micaela, Michaeleen, Michelle

St. Michael the Archangel is one of the three angels mentioned in the Bible, where he is described as the defender of God's people. The Book of Revelation pictures him as leading the heavenly army against Satan and the fallen angels, and driving them from heaven.

Mildred (*Old English:* Mild Strength)

July 13

Other Forms: Melissa, Millie, Milly

St. Mildred was one of the daughters of St. Emenburga of England. She was educated in France and on her return to England became a nun. She eventually became abbess of her monastery, and there is a record of her attending a provincial council in 694. There is no record of the date of her death, but her relics were moved and enshrined at Canterbury in 1030.

Monica (*Greek:* Counselor)

Aug. 27

Other Forms: Mona, Monique

St. Monica (333-387) was born into a Christian family in North Africa. She was married to a pagan, Patricius, who did not lead a good life. Monica attended Mass daily, prayed, and did good works in the hope of converting him. It took many years, but he was at last won over. Monica is best known for her son, Augustine. He was a brilliant boy who became a teacher. Like his father, he did not lead a good life and even became a heretic. Once she went to a bishop to ask him to talk to Augustine, saying she could do nothing but pray. "Keep doing that," the bishop told her. "It is impossible that the son of so many tears will perish." Monica and Augustine went to Milan, Italy, where he was to teach, and there he was converted by St. Ambrose. From then on he and his mother rivaled each other in growing holy. Augustine was preparing to take her back to Africa when she died in Ostia at the age of 56. Augustine went on to become a great saint and Doctor of the Church. He wrote about his mother in his famous book *Confessions.*

71

ST. MONICA

Myra (Feminine of Myron, *Greek:* Fragment)   Aug. 17

St. Myron was a priest in charge of a parish in Greece. During the persecution of Decius, soldiers came to his church to arrest Christians and destroy the church. St. Myron met them and protested the ruling. He was beaten on the spot, arrested, and then executed.

Nadine (*Russian:* Hope)   Aug. 1

Another Form: Nadia

See: Faith

Natalie (*Latin:* Birth)   July 27

Other Forms: Natalia, Natasha, Nathalie

Natalie was a woman servant in the Christian household of St. Hadrian, an officer in the imperial army. When he was arrested and tortured during the persecution of the Emperor Diocletian, Natalie ministered to him and other martyrs in prison before they were put to death. She was spared martyrdom herself and died peacefully in Constantinople about 311 A.D.

Nicole (Feminine of Nicholas,   Dec. 6
Greek: People's Victory)

Other Forms: Nicola, Nicolette

St. Nicholas was one of the most popular saints in the early Church and many legends have grown up about him. One of them tells how he brings presents to children at Christmas (Saint Claus, or Santa Claus). He was the Archbishop of Myra and is patron of children. He died about 324.

Nora (Diminutive of Honorata, *Latin:* Honored)   Jan. 11

Other Forms: Honora, Honorée, Norah, Noreen, Norine

St. Honorata was a nun who lived in the Fifth Century. She was a sister of St. Epiphanius of Parva in Italy. During an invasion of northern tribes, she was taken into captivity. Her brother ransomed her and brought her back to Pavia. She led a very holy life and died about 500 A.D. Many miracles are said to have been worked in her name.

Olga (Russian for Helga, *Norse:* Holy)   July 11

St. Olga was the widowed wife of a Russian grand duke who lived in the region of Kiev. She was one of the first Russians to be baptized. She endeavored to spread her new faith among the Russian people. She died in 969.

Olive (*Latin:* Olive)   June 2

Other Forms: Oliva, Olivia

St. Olive was a holy nun who lived in a convent south of Rome. She is known for a life dedicated to prayer and penance. The dates when she lived are uncertain.

Patricia (Feminine of Patrick,   Mar. 17
Latin: Nobly Born)

St. Patrick is the patron saint of Ireland. Born in Britain about 385, he was captured as a youth and taken as a slave to Ireland. Later he escaped and returned home. The paganism of the Irish people bothered him so he resolved to become a priest and go there to preach the Gospel. When he did return it was as a bishop. Despite early difficulties, he was remarkably successful. He organized the Church in Ireland, lived a life of prayer and penance, dying in 461.

Paula (Feminine of Paul, from *Latin:* Little)   June 29

Other Forms: Paulette, Pauline

St. Paul is one of the great figures of Christian history. He was a Roman citizen from Tarsus in Asia Minor. As a young man he went to Jerusalem to study his Jewish religion. He became a hater of Christianity and a persecutor of the Jews. He was present at the stoning of St. Stephen and was on the way to Damascus to arrest Christians when he was struck to the ground and Christ appeared to him. Jesus asked Paul why he was persecuting Him. From that moment on, Paul became entirely devoted to spreading Christianity. He was beaten and persecuted, but he continued his missionary journeys taking the new faith to Europe. Finally, arrested, he was taken in chains to Rome for trial. Released, he continued his work. During the persecution of Nero, he was rearrested. Because he was a Roman citizen, he was beheaded, not crucified like St. Peter. His death took place in 67 A.D. His writings are found in the Bible, and the account of his missionary work can be read in the Book of Acts.

Other saints with this name:

St. Paula of Rome (Jan. 26)
St. Paula, Martyr (June 3)

Priscilla (*Latin:* Ancient)   Jan. 16

St. Priscilla was a wealthy Roman matron whose son was a senator. Two of her grandchildren are Sts. Praxedes and Pudentiana. Tradition says that she was converted by St. Peter and often had him as guest in her home. She donated part of her property as a burial place (catacomb) for Christians. A Roman church is named after her.

Rafaela (Feminine of Raphael,   Sept. 29
Hebrew: God's Healer)

St. Raphael is one of the three angels mentioned in the Bible. His story may be found in the Book of Tobit.

Ramona (Feminine of Raymond, *Teutonic:* Protector) Aug. 31

Other Forms: Mona, Raimunda

St. Raymond Nonnatus was born in Spain where he joined the newly-founded order of Our Lady of Ransom, which was dedicated to the ransom of captives of the Moors. He went to North Africa to redeem these Christian slaves and gave himself in place of one. After a long period of harsh slavery, he was ransomed by his order. When he returned to Europe, he was made a cardinal. However, he continued to live humbly until his death in 1240.

Rebecca (*Hebrew:* Ensnarer)

Rebecca is a figure of the Old Testament, and there is no saint of the New Law with this name. Rebecca was the daughter of the Patriarch Abraham's nephew, sister of Laban, and she became the bride of Isaac, Abraham's son. She was the mother of Jacob and Esau. You can read her story in the Book of Genesis, particularly Chapters 24 and 25. Because of her deception she was punished by being separated from Jacob. She was buried in the family tomb in Hebron.

Regina (*Latin:* Queen) Aug. 22

Other Forms: Reine, Renée

This is a name given in honor of the Blessed Virgin Mary, Queen of Heaven. There is a special Mass for this feast.

Rita (Form of Margaret, see) May 22

St. Rita was a wife and mother in Cassia, Italy. After eighteen years of married life, she had lost both her husband and children. She joined a convent, and although she suffered ill health which left her in great pain, she was always cheerful and kind. She was a woman of great prayer. St. Rita died in 1456 and is credited with many miracles.

Roberta (Feminine of Robert, *Teutonic:* Bright Flame)

Sept. 17

St. Robert Bellarmine is honored as a Doctor (Teacher) of the Church. He is recognized as one of the great theologians of Christianity. He died in 1621.

Rosaria (*Spanish:* Rosary)

Oct. 7

This is a name given in honor of Our Lady of the Rosary, a title of the Blessed Virgin Mary.

Rose (*Latin:* Rose)

Aug. 23

Other Forms: Rosa, Rosalie, Rosalind, Rosalinda, Rosaline, Rosalyn, Roseanna, Rosemarie, Rosemonde, Rosetta

St. Rose of Lima was born, lived, and died in Lima, Peru. She was christened Isabella, but because of her bright red cheeks, her mother called her Rose. She was a child in love with God. She fasted, did great penances, and is said to have been rewarded with visions and heavenly visits. She had a little house with a tiny room built for her in her parents' garden, put an iron chain around her waist, and had the key to its lock thrown down a well so that it could not be recovered. Although never strong in health, she bore her illnesses without complaint. She died in 1617 and her body was buried in the Dominican church of which she was a member of the Third Order. She is credited with many miracles. She is the patroness of Peru.

ST. ROSALIA

(Sept. 4)

St. Rosalia is the patron saint of Palermo, Sicily. She was a hermit who lived in a cave there and who is noted for her penances. She died in

ST. ROSE OF LIMA

1160 and is celebrated for many miracles which have been attributed to her intercession.

Ruth (*Hebrew:* Female Friend)

Ruth was an outstanding woman of the Old Testament, but there is no saint of the New Law by this name. Her story is contained in the Book of Ruth. She was a Moabite woman who married the son of Naomi. After his death Naomi decided to return to Juda and told Ruth to go back to her people. In one of the most beautiful passages in the Old Testament she decided to stay with Naomi. Ruth went with Naomi to Bethlehem, where she married Booz. Her son, Obed, was the grandfather of David and thus Ruth became an ancestor of Christ. She is a model for relationships between a daughter-in-law and a mother-in-law.

Sabina (*Latin:* Member of the Sabine Tribe)   Aug. 29

Another Form: Savina

St. Sabina was a wealthy Italian widow of Umbria. She was converted to Christianity by her slave, St. Seraphia. After her conversion she adopted Seraphia as a daughter. Both women were put to death for their faith, about 127 A.D.

Sandra (Feminine of Alexander, *Greek:* Helper of Men)

There are a number of saints with the name Alexander (see Alessandra). There was St. Alexander Briant (Dec. 1), an English martyr; St. Alexander of Egypt (Feb. 26); St. Alexander of Jerusalem (Mar. 18); St. Alexander of Constantinople (Aug. 28).

Sarah (*Hebrew: Princess*)

Other Forms: Sally, Sara, Sarai, Shari

Sarah is a Biblical name. Sarah was the wife of the patriarch, Abraham, and the mother of Isaac. Her story is in the Book of Genesis. Sarah has never been defined by the Church as a saint. The only saint with this name is St. Sara (July 13), who during the Fourth Century lived the life of a hermit on the banks of the Nile.

Selma (Feminine of Anselm,   Apr. 21
Teutonic: Divine Helmet)

St. Anselm is a Doctor (Teacher) of the Church. He was born in Italy in 1033 but as a young man went to France, where he became a monk. In 1093 he was appointed Archbishop of Canterbury (England), but he was twice driven into exile for defending the rights of the Church against English kings. He died at Canterbury in 1109, leaving behind many writings in philosophy which have given him his reputation as a scholar.

Serafina (*Hebrew:* Burning)

Other Forms: Fina, Seraphia, Seraphina

This name is taken from the name of a group of angels who stand before the throne of God (the seraphim). The feast of the Guardian Angels (Oct. 2) can be used. Blessed Seraphina Sforza (Sept. 8) suffered much abuse from a cruel husband. Later she entered the Franciscan Sisters where she came to lead her community. She died in 1478. St. Seraphia was the adopted daughter of St. Sabina (see). She was beheaded for her religion in 122. Her feast is July 29.

Sharon (From *Hebrew:* Plain)

This name is taken from a title of the Blessed Virgin Mary: Rose of Sharon. Any one of her feast days can be used by those with this name, although Sept. 12 seems most appropriate. See: Mary.

Silvia (*Latin:* Of the Forest) Nov. 3

Other Forms: Sylva, Sylvaine, Sylvette, Sylvia, Sylvie

St. Sylvia was the mother of Pope St. Gregory the Great. She is held up both as a model of widowhood and a Christian mother. She lived in the Sixth Century and the exact year of her death is unknown.

Simone (Feminine of Simon, *Hebrew:* Obedient) Oct. 28

Other Forms: Simona, Mona

St. Simon was one of the Twelve Apostles. He is also known as St. Simon the Zealot, after a group to which he had belonged. After the death of Christ he is said to have preached the Gospel first in North Africa and then in Persia and Mesopotamia, in which region he was put to death for his preaching.

Solange (*Old French:* Earth-Angel) May 10

Solange was a shepherdess of Burges, France. A beautiful girl, she worked hard and was of a lovable disposition. A young nobleman of the region saw her and wanted her for himself. Solange, however, had promised to remain a virgin out of love of God. The young nobleman had no success in courting her, so he resolved to kidnap her. He tried to drag her away, but she fought so desperately that he lost his temper and killed her with his sword. She died about 844.

Sophia (*Greek:* Wisdom)

Other Forms: Nadia, Nadine, Sofia, Sonia, Sonya, Sophie

The Eastern Church has great devotion to the Holy Wisdom (Sancta Sophia) of God and one of the world's greatest basilicas was built under this title in Constantinople. Many children are named after this title of God.

ST. TERESA OF AVILA

ST. SOPHIA (Sept. 30)

Legend says St. Sophia was the mother of Sts. Faith (see), Hope and Charity, who were martyred in Rome in the Second Century. She is said to have died shortly after, while praying at their tomb.

Stella (*Latin:* Star)

Other Forms: Estella, Estelle, Estrella, Estrellita (see Esther)

This name was originally given after a name for Mary in the Litany of the Blessed Virgin, *Stella Maris* or Star of the Sea. Any of her feasts may be used as a name day (see: Mary).

Stephanie (Feminine of Stephen, *Greek:* Crowned)

Dec. 26

Other Forms: Esta, Estancia, Stefanie

St. Stephen was the first martyr of the Church. He was a deacon who was stoned to death outside the walls of Jerusalem. His story can be read in the Bible in the sixth and seventh chapters of the Book of Acts.

Susanna (*Hebrew:* Lily)

Aug. 11

Other Forms: Susan, Suzanne, Suzette

Susanna was a Roman maiden of noble birth. She is said to have been a niece of Pope St. Caius. When she refused to marry a pagan, a relative of the Emperor Diocletian, because she was a Christian, she was arrested and put to death about the year 190. A popular church in Rome bears her name.

Theodora (Feminine of Theodore, *Greek:* God's Gift)

Other Forms: Dolly, Dora, Dorothy (see), Theodosia

ST. THEODORA, VIRGIN AND MARTYR (Apr. 1)

St. Theodora was a young woman who lived in Rome with her brother, St. Hermes. Both of them were arrested as Christians under the Emperor Hadrian and put to death A.D. 132.

ST. THEODORA, PENITENT (Sept. 11)

St. Theodora lived in Alexandria, Egypt, in the Fifth Century. As a young woman she led a sinful life. She was converted, and from then on her life was one of penance and sacrifice. She is said to have lived to an old age.

ST. THEODORA, MATRON (Sept. 17)

St. Theodora was a well-to-do Roman woman of high birth who was a Christian. During the persecution of Diocletian she took it upon herself to give aid and comfort to Christians who were imprisoned, and to rescue their bodies for Christian burial after their execution. She was never arrested herself and is said to have died in 305 A.D.

Theresa (*Greek:* Reaper)

Other Forms: Teresa, Terese, Terry, Thérèse, Tracy

ST. THERESE (Oct. 1)

St. Thérèse of the Child Jesus, also known as the Little Flower, was born in France in 1873. She was one of five daughters, all of whom became nuns. As a child she was very religious. When she was fifteen, she entered the Carmelite convent in Lisieux, declaring she wanted to save souls and pray for priests. She worked at various tasks in the convent and did not seem extraordinary. She kept a sort of diary which was published after her death under the title *The Story of a Soul.* This book showed her spiritual greatness and won her a large following. She said she wanted to become a

ST. THERESE OF LISIEUX

saint by doing ordinary things. "Even to pick up a pin can convert a soul," she wrote. The book also showed the spiritual suffering she endured, often feeling abandoned by God. She died after a painful illness in 1897. She had written: "I want to spend my heaven doing good on earth." She also promised that after death she would send a shower of roses on earth, and many people's lives have been changed by this simple young nun. Because she prayed for missioners, she has been named patroness of the missions.

ST. TERESA (Oct. 15)

St. Teresa, one of the great women of the Church, a Doctor (Teacher) of the Church, was born in Avila, Spain, in 1515. When she was seven years old, she ran away to join the Moors because she thought they would cut off her head and she could become a martyr. Returned home safely, she built a hermitage in her parents' garden, where she pretended she was a hermit. She joined the Carmelite Convent in Avila, where she decided that she owed her whole self to God. From that time on her life was filled with prayer, visions, and sufferings. She reformed the Carmelite order and had the help of another great mystic, St. John of the Cross. She founded thirty-five convents. Once she said she was beginning a new convent, although she only had three ducats. Friends told her it was impossible with so little money. She replied: "Teresa and three ducats are nothing, but Teresa, three ducats, and God can make a success of anything." Her writings on mystical prayer are still considered the best books on the subject that were ever written. She died in ecstasy, looking at a crucifix, in 1582.

Thomasina (Feminine of Thomas, *Aramaic:* Twin) July 3

Other Forms: Tomasa, Tomasina, Tomasine

There are a large number of saints named Thomas, all of whom derive their name from St. Thomas the Apostle. He is the Apostle who doubted the Resurrection of Jesus and said he would not believe unless he could put his hands on the wounds. A week later Jesus reappeared and called Thomas to come and touch His wounds, saying, "Do not be faithless but believing." According to tradition, St. Thomas went as far as India preaching the Gospel, and it was there that he was martyred. He is patron for architects and masons.

Trinidad (*Spanish:* Trinity)

Trinidad is a popular name among the Spanish-speaking and is given in honor of the Holy Trinity. This is a movable feast that comes the Sunday after Pentecost.

Ursula (*Latin:* Little Bear)   Oct. 21

St. Ursula is said to have been the daughter of a Briton chief. When the Saxons invaded England, St. Ursula led a band of British maidens in an escape to Europe. The group landed near the mouth of the Rhine River, where they were put to death by pagan Huns. A shrine in Cologne is said to contain their bones. St. Ursula was named patroness of school teachers.

Valery (Feminine of Valerian, *Latin:* Brave)   Dec. 9

Other Forms: Valeria, Valerie

St. Valery was born in Limoges, France, sometime in the third century. She was converted by St. Martial. She is said to have been beheaded for being a Christian. Nothing else is known of her.

Veronica (*Greek:* Victory Bringer)   Feb. 4

Other Forms: Bernice, Vera, Veronique

Veronica is the name given traditionally to the woman who, taking her head covering, used it to wipe the face of Jesus while He was carrying His cross to Calvary. When she received it back, it was said to be imprinted with the suffering face of Jesus (Veronica's Veil). Her deed is commemorated in the Sixth Station of the Cross.

Victoria (*Latin:* Victory)   Dec. 23

St. Victoria was a Roman virgin. She was arrested as a Christian during the persecution of Decius (250 A.D.) and ordered to either sacrifice to

87

idols or marry a pagan husband. She refused both and was stabbed to death.

Vincentia (Feminine of Vincent, Latin: Conquering) June 4

Another Form: Vincenza

St. Vincenza Gerosa (1784-1847) was the foundress of the Sisters of Charity of Lovere (Brescia, Italy) who devoted their services to the education of girls and the care of the sick. The foundation grew rapidly and spread throughout the world.

This name is also given in honor of St. Vincent de Paul (Sept. 27) or St. Vincent Ferrer (Apr. 5).

Virginia (Latin: Virgin)

A name given in honor of the Blessed Virgin Mary. Any one of her feast days can be chosen as a name day.

Vivian (From Bibiana, Latin: Lively) Dec. 2

St. Bibiana belonged to a Christian family in Rome during the reign of Julian the Apostate, emperor from 355 to 361. Her father, who had been prefect of Rome, was branded and sold as a slave. Her mother was beheaded. Bibiana was tied to a pillar and beaten with lead-weighted scourges until she died.

Wilhelmina (Feminine of Wilhelm, German for William, Teutonic: Strong Helmet)

There are a number of saints by the name of William. One of them, William of Roskilde, was an Englishman who was chaplain to King

Canute. Concerned about the welfare of the people of Denmark, he went there as a missioner. His life of zeal and piety won many people who after his death praised him as a saint. He died in 1067. His feast day is Sept. 2.

Winifred (Form of Genevieve, Celtic: White Wave) Nov. 3

St. Winifred is one of the patrons of Wales. She was guided in her faith by St. Beuno. She was put to death by Caradoc, a Seventh Century tyrant, at a place since called Holywell where many miracles have occurred.

Yvette (Form of Judith, Hebrew: Praised) Jan. 13

Another Form: Yvonne

Blessed Yvette lived for forty years as a wife and mother and then spent the next thirty dwelling in a small cell built near the church of Huy. One of her sons became an abbot in Luxemburg. She persuaded her father to become a monk. Before she retired to her cell, Yvette had worked among lepers. She died in 1228.

Zita (Italian: Little Hope) Apr. 27

St. Zita had as her motto, "Do what pleases God, avoid what displeases Him." She came from a poor family and had to work hard as a child. When she was eighteen, she became a servant in a rich family's home, where she remained until she died in 1271. She arose very early to attend Mass before her work began, saved her food to give to the poor, was always smiling and cheerful, and, when abused by fellow workers who were jealous of her holiness, she returned some kindness. She did nothing great by worldly standards but did become a great saint. She is patroness of maids and other domestic workers.

Zoe (*Hebrew:* Life)   July 5

St. Zoe was the wife of a high Roman official. Despite his position, she was arrested for being a Christian. After being hung from a tree and a fire lit under her feet, she was suffocated. She died about 286.

Part Two:

Names in This Book

There are thousands of saints who are not in this book. If your name is not included below, however, there is a good chance it is not a saint's name. It may be a nickname or part of a name; very few of those are in this book. If you were named Angie, Cindy, Debbie, or Linda, for example, look under Angela, Cynthia, Diana, or Lucinda, Deborah, Melanie, or Rose. It may be a made-up name, a family name, or a name from popular, non-Christian mythology. If your first name is not included below, you may "adopt" a patron saint whose name sounds like yours.

Abigail . . . . page 11
Abbie 11
Abby 11
Ada 11
Adalberta 11
Adalie 11
Adela 11
Adelaide 11
Adele 11
Adelheid 11
Adelina 11
Adeline 11

Adria 13
Adriana 13
Adrienne 13
Agatha 13
Agathe 13
Agathy 13
Agnella 13
Agnes .... 13, 28; *picture,* 12
Agnete 13
Agnita 13
Aileen 52
Aimee 15
Alba 14
Alberta 14
Albertina 14
Albina 14
Alene 52
Alessandra 14, 79
Aleth 14
Alex 14
Alexandra 14
Alexandrina 14
Alexis 14
Aleydis 14
Alfreda 45
Alfrida 45
Alice 14
Alicia 14
Aline 11, 52
Alisa 14
Alise 34-38
Alison 14, 60
Alix 14
Aliza 34-38
Alma 15
Aloysia 60
Althryda 45
Alyce 14
Alys 14
Amanda 15
Amata 15
Amelia 38
Amy 15
Anastasia 15
Andrea 17
Angel 17
Angela 17
Angelica 17
Angelina 17
Angelique 17
Angelita 17
Anita 17
Ann .... 17; *picture,* 16
Anna 17

Annabel 17
Annabella 17
Anne 17
Annette 17
Antoinette 18
Antonia 18
Antonina 18
Arlene 22
Arlette 22
Audrey 18, 39
Babette 34-38
Barbara 18
Beatrice 18
Beatrix 18
Beatriz 18
Bella 34-38
Belle 34-38
Bernadette .... 19, 27; *picture*, 20
Bernardine 19
Bernice 19, 87
Berta 19
Bertha 19
Bertild 19
Bertilla 19
Bess 34-38
Bessie 34-38
Beth 34-38
Betsy 34-38
Bette 34-38
Betty 34-38
Bianca 14
Bibiana 88
Birgit 21
Blanche 14, 47
Brenda 19
Bride 21
Bridget 21
Bridie 21
Bridig 21
Briel 45-47
Brigid 21
Brigida 21
Brigit 21
Brigitta 21
Brigitte 21
Caecilia 24
Camelia 21
Camilla 21
Camille 21
Cara 24
Carey 22
Carla 22
Carmel 21-22, 68
Carmelita 21-22

93

Carmella 21-22
Carol 22
Carola 22
Carole 22
Caroline 22
Cassandra 14
Catalina 22
Caterina 22
Catherine .... 21, 57; *picture,* 23
Cecile 24
Cecilia 24
Cecily 24
Ceil 24
Celine 52
Cesca 43-45
Chantale 24
Charity 24, 42, 83
Charlene 22
Charlotte 22
Cheryl 22
Chiara 25
Christiana 24
Christina 24
Christine 24
Cicely 24
Cicily 24
Claire 25
Clairette 25
Clara 25
Clare .... 25, 27, 55; *picture,* 26
Clareta 25
Clarice 25
Clarissa 25
Clarita 25
Claudette 25
Claudia 25
Claudine 25
Clemence 25
Clementia 25
Clementina 25
Clementine 25
Coleen 27
Colette 27
Colleen 27
Colombina 27
Columba 27
Columbia 27
Columbina 27
Columbine 27
Concepcion 27
Concepta 27
Conception 27, 68
Consolata 28
Constance 28

Constantia 28
Constanza 28
Consuela 28
Consuelo 28
Cora 28
Cornelia 28
Cynthia 28, 30
Danette 29
Daniela 29
Danielle 29
Daria 29
Darlene 29
Debora 29
Deborah 29
Debra 29
Della 11
Denise 29
Diana 30
Diane 30
Dinah 30
Dolly 84
Dolor 30
Dolores 30, 68
Dolorita 30
Dominga 30
Dominica 30
Dominique 30
Domitilla 30
Dona 32
Donata 32
Donatilla 32
Donna 32
Dora 32, 84
Doreen 32
Doris 32
Dorotea 32
Dorothea 32
Dorothy .... 32, 84; *picture,* 31
Eadie 32-34
Eda 32-34
Edissa 39
Edith 32-34
Edna 34
Edwina 34
Edythe 32-34
Eileen 52
Elain 52
Elaine 52
Elane 52
Eleanor 34
Eleanore 52
Elena 52
Elenord 34
Eleonore 34

Elinor 34
Elisa 34-38
Elise 34-38
Elissa 14
Eliza 34-38
Elizabeth .... 34-38; *pictures,* 33, 35, 37
Ella 52
Ellen 52
Eloisa 60
Eloise 60
Elsa 34-38
Else 14,   34-38
Elsie 34-38
Emelie 38
Emeline 38
Emenburga 71
Emilia 38
Emiliana 38
Emily 38
Emma 38
Enrica 38
Erica 38
Erika 38
Erma 55
Ernestine 39
Esperanza 39
Esta 83
Estancia 83
Estella 83
Estelle 83
Esther 39, 83
Estrella 83
Estrellita 83
Ethel 39
Etheldra 18, 39
Etheldreda 39
Ethelreda 39
Eugenia 39-40
Eugenie 39-40
Eulalia 40
Eulalie 40
Eunice 40
Eva 40
Eve 40
Eveline 40
Evelyn 40
Evita 40
Fabiola 40
Faith 24, 39, 42, 52, 73, 83
Fanchon 43-45
Fanny 43-45
Fay 42
Fe 42
Felice 42

Felicia 42
Felicienne 42
Felicita 42
Felicitas 42
Felicity 42
Felipa 42
Fenna 43-45
Fidelia 42
Fina 80
Fleur 43
Flora 43
Florence 43
Florentia 43
Florentina 43
Florentine 43
France 43-45
Frances .... 43-45; *pictures,* 41, 44
Francesca 43-45
Franchette 43-45
Francine 43-45
Francoise 43-45
Frannie 43-45
Freda 45
Frederica 45
Frederika 45
Gabriela 45-47
Gabriella 45-47
Gabrielle 45-47
Gail 11
Gale 11
Gemma 47
Genevieve .... 47, 57, 89; *picture,* 46
Georgana 47-48
Georgette 47-48
Georgia 47-48
Georgianna 47-48
Geralda 48
Geraldine 48
Geralyn 48
Gerda 50
Germaine .... 48; *picture,* 49
Gertrude 50
Gina 39-40
Ginette 47
Giovanna 55-57
Giuseppina 58
Gladys 50
Gloria 50
Grace 50
Greta 64-66
Gretchen 64-66
Guadaloupe 50-51
Guadalupe 50-51
Gwen 51

97

Gwendoline 51
Hally 51
Hannah 17
Harietta 51
Harriet 38, 51
Harriette 51
Helen 34, 52
Helena .... 52; *picture,* 53
Helene 52
Helga 74
Heloise 60
Henrietta 38, 51
Henriette 51
Hilda 52
Hildegarde 52
Honora 74
Honorata 74
Honorée 74
Hope 42, 52, 83
Ida 54
Ignatia 54
Illse 14
Ilona 52
Ilsa 14
Immaculata 54
Ines 13
Inez 13
Irena 54
Irene 54
Irma 55
Irmina 55
Irmine 55
Isabel 34-38
Isabella 34-38
Isobel 34-38
Jacoba 55
Jacqueline 55
Jane 55-57
Janet 55-57
Janice 55-57
Jean 55-57
Jeanette 55-57
Jeanine 55-57
Jeanne 55-57
Jennifer 57
Jessica 55-57
Jessie 55-57
Jill 58
Joan .... 55-57; *picture,* 56
Jo Ann 55-57
Joanna 55-57
Joanne 55-57
Johanna 55-57
Josefa 58

Josepha 58
Josephine 58
Josette 58
Josianne 58
Juana 55-57
Juanita 55-57
Judith 58, 89
Judy 58
Julia 58
Juliana 58
Julianna 58
Julie 58
Juliet 58
Juliette 58
June 55-57
Justa 59
Justina 59
Justine 59
Karen 22
Kate 22
Kateri 22
Katherine 22
Kathleen 22
Kathryn 22
Katrina 22
Kay 22
Kirsten 24
Kit 22
Kitty 22
Klementine 25
Konstanze 28
Kristin 24
Lara 59
Laraine 59
Laura 59
Laureen 59
Laurenta 59
Laurentia 59
Laurette 59
Leanore 34
Lee 34-38, 59
Lena 52
Lenora 34
Lenore 34, 52
Leona 59
Leonie 59
Leonita 59
Leora 34
Lila 59
Lilian 34-38, 59
Lillian 59
Lily 59
Lisa 34-38
Lisabeth 34-38

Lisbeth 34-38
Lise 34-38
Lisette 34-38
Lison 34-38
Lois 60
Lola 30
Lolita 30
Loretta 59
Lorraine 59
Louisa 60
Louise 60
Luc 60
Luce 60
Lucette 60
Lucia 60
Lucie 60
Lucien 60
Lucienne 60
Lucilla 60
Lucille 60
Lucina 18
Lucinda 60
Lucy .... 60; *picture,* 61
Luisa 60
Luise 60
Lupe 50-51
Luz 60
Lydia 62
Mabel 62
Maddalena 62
Madeline 62
Madge 64-66
Mae 68
Magda 62
Magdalene .... 62, 66, 68; *picture,* 63
Maggie 64-66
Maime 68
Maisie 64-66
Manuela 62
Mara 68
Marcelina 64
Marcella 64
Marcelle 64
Marcia 64
Margaret .... 64-66, 76-77; *picture,* 65
Margarita 64-66
Marge 64-66
Margery 64-66
Margo 64-66
Margot 64-66
Marguerite 64-66
Maria 68
Marian 68
Marianna 68

Maribel 68
Marie 68
Marietta 68
Mariette 68
Marigold 68
Marilyn 68
Marina 64-66
Marjorie 64-66
Marlene 62
Marsha 64
Marta 66
Martha .... 66; *picture*, 67
Marthe 66
Martina 66
Martine 66
Mary ... 15, 17, 19, 21-22, 27, 30, 34, 36, 50-51, 58, 62, 68, 70, 76, 77, 80, 83, 88; *picture*, 69
Marya 68
Mathilde 70
Matilda 70
Maud 70
Maude 70
Maura 70
Maureen 68
May 68
Melania 70
Melanie 70
Melinda 70
Melissa 71
Merced 70
Mercedes 68, 70
Mercy 70
Micaela 71
Michaela 71
Michaeleen 71
Michelle 71
Mildred 71
Millie 71
Milly 71
Mirelle 68
Miriam 68
Moira 68
Molly 68
Mona 71, 76, 81
Monica .... 71; *picture*, 72
Monique 71
Myra 73
Nadia 73, 81-83
Nadine 19, 73, 81-83
Nan 17
Nancy 17
Nanette 17
Natalia 73
Natalie 73
Natasha 73

Nathalie 73
Nell 34, 52
Nellie 34, 52
Nelly 34
Neysa 13
Nicola 73
Nicole 73
Nicolette 73
Nina 13, 24
Ninette 13
Niñon 17
Nita 55-57
Nora 74
Norah 74
Noreen 74
Norine 74
Odilla 51
Olga 74
Oliva 74
Olive 74
Olivia 74
Palatias 59
Patricia 74
Paula 75
Paulette 75
Pauline 75
Pearl 64-66
Pegeen 64-66
Peggy 64-66
Perpetua 42
Polly 68
Praxedes 75
Priscilla 75
Pudentiana 75
Rachel 13
Rafaela 75
Raimunda 76
Ramona 76
Rebecca 76
Regina 76
Reine 76
Renata 54
Renée 54, 76
Rita 64-66, 76-77
Roberta 77
Rosa 77-79
Rosalia 77-79
Rosalie 77-79
Rosalind 77-79
Rosalinda 77-79
Rosaline 77-79
Rosalyn 77-79
Rosaria 68, 77
Rose .... 77-79; picture, 78

Roseanna 77-79
Rosemarie 77-79
Rosemonde 77-79
Rosetta 77-79
Ruth 79
Sabina 79, 80
Sally 80
Sandra 14, 79
Sara 80
Sarah 80
Sarai 80
Savina 79
Selina 52
Seline 52
Selma 80
Serafina 80
Seraphia 79, 80
Seraphina 80
Shari 80
Sharon 80
Sheila 24
Silvia 81
Simona 81
Simone 81
Sofia 81-83
Solange 81
Sonia 81-83
Sonya 81-83
Sophia 42, 81-83
Sophie 81-83
Stacey 15
Stasia 15
Stathia 15
Statia 15
Stefanie 83
Stella 83
Stephanie 83
Susan 83
Susanna 83
Suzanne 83
Suzette 83
Sylva 81
Sylvaine 81
Sylvette 81
Sylvia 81
Sylvie 81
Tanya 18
Teresa .... 84-86; *picture,* 82
Terese 84-86
Terry 84-86
Theodora 32, 84
Theodosia 84
Theresa 84-86
Thérèse .... 84-86; *picture,* 85

103

Thomasina 86
Tilda 70
Tillie 70
Tina 24, 59
Tomasa 86
Tomasina 86
Tomasine 86
Toni 18
Tonia 18
Tracy 84-86
Trina 22
Trinidad 87
Trudy 50
Ursula 17, 87
Valeria 87
Valerie 87
Valery 87
Vanessa 39
Vera 87
Veronica 87
Veronique 87
Victoria 87-88
Vincentia 88
Vincenza 88
Violane 47
Virginia 88
Vivian 88
Wilfrida 32-34
Wilhelmina 88-89
Winifred 89
Wulfridis 32-34
Yolanda 47
Yvette 58, 89
Yvonne 89
Zita 89
Zoe 90